Terry!
The Louvre is an
awesome experience.
He wish it for
you. Love Mom & Dad
May 1997

THE LOUVRE

ARCHITECTURE AND HISTORY

First published in Great Britain in 1995 by
Thames and Hudson Ltd, London

© Text and photos Editions Assouline, Paris, 1995

British Library Cataloguing-in-Publication Data

A catalogue record for this book is available from the British Library

ISBN 0-500-34140-0

Printed and bound in Italy

THE LOUVRE

ARCHITECTURE AND HISTORY

Genevieve Bresc Bautier

Photographs by Keiichi Tahara

THAMES AND HUDSON

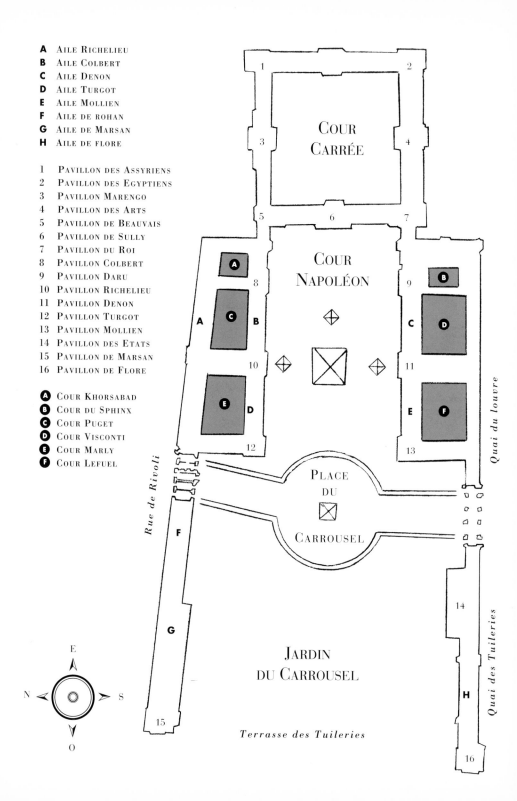

Cour Carrée

Cour Napoléon

Quai du louvre

Rue de Rivoli

Place du Carrousel

Jardin du Carrousel

Quai des Tuileries

Terrasse des Tuileries

E
N — S
O

The Great Tower
of the Louvre

The term "Louvre" was first used in the late 12th century and designated an area west of Paris, the city which, under Philip Augustus, was forging its way to becoming the capital of France.

In 1190, before Philip Augustus set off for the Crusade with his brother-in-law, Richard the Lion Heart, King of England, he decided to protect the city of Paris and the royal palace that would be in an extremely vulnerable position if attacked by invaders from the west. According to his biographer, Rigord, he ordered his burghers to build a wall around the city; known as the wall of Philip Augustus, it separated the residential areas from the "faubourgs", including the Louvre quarter where houses and a church had already been built.

At the junction of the city wall and the River Seine a mighty fortress known as the Tour du Louvre, the "Louvre tower", was built. The first reference to the tower is found in 1202. So impressive was the tower that it was promptly copied and similar plans used for another royal castle, Dun-le-Roi. The tower was a sturdy four-sided construction (72 m x 78 m) (235 ft x 255 ft), surrounded by a moat filled with water from the Seine. It was defended by four circular corner-towers and semi-circular flanking towers either side of the entrance gates. The unusual feature of the castle was its very compact appearance: there was no bailey, chapel or secondary buildings except for two small houses, to the south and west, and the "great tower" or keep in the middle, a perfect circle placed slightly off-centre and surrounded by another (dry) moat.

Archaeological research carried out in 1984 and 1985 by Michel Fleury and Venceslas Kruta uncovered the basic structure of the mighty fortress and the walls constructed by workers who had left their mark carved into the blocks of white stone. The moats of the medieval Louvre can now be viewed when visiting the museum.

t he Tour du Louvre, like the Tower of London, was a castle built for defence purposes, standing on the river outside the city. It was a fortress on a fall-back position, with wells to supply water and the capacity to withstand a siege. It could also be used as a prison or vault. By this time a number of assemblies had been held at the Louvre, probably in the Great Hall, the same one that came to be known as the Hall of Saint Louis during the reign of Charles V. The walls of the lower hall were built at the time of Philip Augustus. In the middle of the 13th century the old ceiling was replaced by a ribbed vault.

The Hall, which was rediscovered during excavations in 1882, features columns with sculpted capitals and all the austere grandeur of medieval residences, although the effect is offset by a touch of humour which grimaces from the springing of the arches.

The Castle of Charles V

by the time Étienne Marcel led the uprisings in Paris, the city had grown and people had moved into the Louvre quarter. In 1358, to protect the city, Marcel had earthworks excavated, forming a wall to the west of the expanding area.

When Charles V gained control of the kingdom, he completed the work, building what was then known as the wall of Charles V. It was a wide defensive earthwork set in front of a deep moat filled with water from the Seine. Archaeological digs conducted by Paul van Ossel in 1990 made it possible to study this vast construction, which was rebuilt in the early 16th century. The 16th-century wall can now be seen in the Carrousel area of the Louvre. Clearly, by this time the Louvre no longer commanded a key position for the defence of the city.

The palace became one of the residences of Charles V. The few documents on the Louvre dating from this period show it standing opposite the city in splendid isolation, shining white, decked with towers and turrets.

Charles V had his master of works, Raymond du Temple, carry out various changes so that the fortress could be inhabited. New houses were built; alternating bedrooms and halls were arranged for the King and Queen; large windows were opened in the walls; a chapel was installed. The tower once used as a falcon house became a library to house part of the vast royal book collections. The floors were laid with terracotta tiles proudly exhibiting royal coats of arms.

The staircase, cantilevered above the space left by the moat in front of the keep, led to the level reserved for the nobility. It was a masterpiece designed by Raymond du Temple (1364–69). On the grand spiral stood statues of the King, the Queen and the King's brothers.

The Renaissance Palace

t he late Middle Ages were not kind to the Louvre, which was forsaken in favour of the Loire valley châteaux. Francis I no doubt considered it drab and dingy and in 1528 he had the great tower demolished. At the end of his reign, in 1546, he commissioned the architect, Pierre Lescot, to design major changes to the palace. On the site of the western residence, a new group of buildings were to be erected, standing symbolically within the confines of the original building.

Henry II later completed the work begun by his father, with only minor and partial changes: the staircase designed for the centre of the residence was transferred further north and a huge hall thus created. Lescot built the "Henry II wing" and a right-angled staircase beneath a superbly sculpted vaulted ceiling. The entire ground floor was taken up by the Great Hall, one side being a "tribunal" reserved for the King, the other a stage for musicians supported by four huge stone caryatids. These ambitious sculptures were the work of Jean Goujon, an architect and sculptor renowned for his illustrations of the works of Vitruvius and his theoretical works on ancient architecture. The sculptures reflected his taste, being both classical and highly decorative.

On the outside, the Henry II wing was designed along both horizontal and vertical lines with three clearly delineated levels: semi-circular arches on the ground floor, one upper storey with imposing windows and an attic storey, ornately decorated with large pediments framing figures and trophies sculpted by Jean Goujon. Three parts projecting from the building were decorated with columns and small circular windows known as bull's-eyes, on which allegories of Peace were sculpted in delicate relief, once again by Jean Goujon; these burst forth in three dimensions, in contrast with the two sections behind. Goujon, who worked on the construction of the Louvre from

1548 to 1562, was an invaluable partner and, together with Lescot, virtually the co-creator of the elaborate relief work on the highly decorated façade, an outstanding example of sculpture that has never been surpassed in the history of French architecture. The iconography of the figures depicted reflects Henry II's vision of the empire. It also illustrates a philosophical concept of royal power as the champion of divine order: the role of the monarchy was that of mediator between the subjects and the world of nature and knowledge.

At the southern corner of the Henry II wing, Lescot built the King's Pavilion overlooking the river, then proceeded to demolish the southern side of the medieval fortress, replacing it with a new wing built at the same level as the other wing. Inside the King's Pavilion was the royal chamber with an ornate wooden ceiling that was the work of Scibecq de Carpi. Later, at the time of the Restoration, it was transferred to a room in the Colonnade. An antechamber with a similarly sculpted ceiling has survived untouched. In 1954, Georges Braque's *Les Oiseaux* was hung there.

This was the palace in which the destiny of the Valois family was played out. It was a venue for celebrations and marriages; it was here that Henry of Navarre married Marguerite of France (the couple later known as King Henry IV and Queen Margot); the processions of Henry III passed here. In 1572 the fearful St Bartholomew's Day Massacre took place at the Louvre; it also witnessed the wars of religion, the flight of Henry III on the day of the barricades (1588) and the excesses of the Holy League.

Work on the palace, or rather the palaces, was never completed. Catherine de' Medici, the Queen Mother, had ordered a new castle to be built — the Tuileries, named after the tile-making workshops ("tuile" = "tile") that previously stood on the site. The architects appointed were Philibert de l'Orme and later Jean Bullant, but their projects were never completed. In 1566 the same fate befell the grand plan of Charles IX to build two galleries, the Petite Galerie between the King's Pavilion and the Seine, and another gallery to connect the Louvre to the Tuileries.

The Grand Plan
of Henry IV

henry IV, entering the conquered city of Paris in 1594, intended to make the Louvre his grand residence, although he also spent a great deal of time and effort on embellishments to the residences at Saint Germain and Fontainebleau. His plan was to make the small quadrangle in the Louvre four times larger and to link the Louvre to the Tuileries by adding two long wings connected to a network of courtyards.

The architects appointed, Louis Metezeau and Androuet du Cerceau, never had time to fulfil the royal ambition. The assassination of the King in 1610 brought work to an abrupt halt. They first built the Petite Galerie, then the Grande Galerie along the Seine to meet up with a new pavilion adjoining the southern end of the Tuileries palace. In the reign of Louis XIV this was named the "Pavillon de Flore".

Henry IV introduced two institutions to the Louvre that would play a major role in the future. A hall panelled in coloured marble was chosen to house the finest antiquities in the royal collections; known as the "hall of antiquities", it may be considered an illustrious ancestor of the Louvre collections today. In 1608 the King had a set of workshops built on the mezzanine level of the Grande Galerie. This provided accommodation for artists with royal appointments and for royal protégés, including not only painters and sculptors but also artisans.

Under the rule of Marie de' Medici work on the Louvre came to a halt and it was not until much later that Louis XIII resurrected his father's projects. In 1628, no doubt encouraged by Richelieu, he decided to lay the foundation stone for a new pavilion at the far end of the Henry II wing, but it was only completed and decorated in 1639–40 under the supervision of the architect Jacques Le Mercier. The pavilion and the adjoining wing followed the lines of the façade designed by Pierre Lescot. But at the very top was a novel and monumental sculpture by Jacques Sarazin: four double groups of caryatids were composed of sensually sculpted female figures. Louis XIII also embarked on the decoration of the Grande Galerie which had been left empty. He brought Nicolas Poussin from Rome and commissioned him to create an ambitious project along the lines of the grand Roman palaces. But the artist soon returned to Rome, abandoning the ceiling where he had originally intended to paint the labours of Hercules.

Transformations under Louis XIV

With a new regent came renewed neglect for the Louvre. However, in 1654 the Court returned to the palace and, at the suggestion of Mazarin, work started once more. The apartments of the Queen Mother on the ground floor of the south wing and the Petite Galerie were lavishly decorated. What remains today is the ambitious ornamentation of the summer apartment of Anne of Austria: the vestibule, adjoining antechamber and bedroom have superb ceilings painted by the Roman artist, Romanelli, surrounded by white and gold stucco work added by Michel Anguier between 1656 and 1658. All that remains of the decoration of the King's apartment is the original ceiling in the bedroom: a vast oval of gilded wood held aloft by captives in chains.

Louis XIV thus pursued the great design of his grandfather. The architect

Le Vau first rebuilt the upper level in the Petite Galerie which had been burnt down in 1661 and added a parallel wing; this façade can still be seen in the Cour du Sphinx. The artist Le Brun devised, painted and sculpted the decoration for the new Petite Galerie: the subject chosen was the sun, the muses and the path of the celestial body through space and time.

Here, with the Galerie d'Apollon, began the emergence of an aesthetic style that would reach its apogee in Versailles. While the original paintings by Le Brun have suffered greatly with the passage of time (and were completed in the 18th and 19th centuries), the stucco work by François Girardon, the Marsy brothers and Thomas Regnaudin is in surprisingly good condition.

Le Vau next set to work on the Louvre quadrangle to make it four times the original size, ultimately producing the Cour Carrée (square courtyard). On the fourth side, overlooking the city, the King and Colbert wanted a majestic façade as a symbol of grandeur. French and Italian architects proposed different solutions.

It was the arrogant Bernini, then at the peak of his fame, who designed the most grandiose palace. He was brought to Paris in 1665, housed, entertained and indulged, before setting to work. However, the French disapproved of the intruder and Colbert set to studying the project with all the fervour of a zealous servant of the state. Bernini soon returned to Rome and the King's builders filed the project away.

A commission of architects, led by a jack-of-all trades by the name of Claude Perrault, was set up. Finding inspiration in projects submitted prior to Bernini's, they built the monumental façade of the Colonnade. The "noble level" featured double columns, a central pavilion and pediment. As the Colonnade was wider than the span of the buildings on the Cour Carrée, the architect had to make the south wing on the Seine twice as deep.

Suddenly work simply stopped. Louis XIV, who had lived in the Louvre for so many years and had enjoyed a wide variety of entertainment (Molière performed in the Caryatid Hall, while the machinery room at the Tuileries, built by Vigarini, was the hall used for large-scale performances), decided to leave Paris, despite the attraction of the Tuileries gardens Le Nôtre had designed for him. There was just not enough space.

With no hunting and with memories of his mother's death at the Louvre, plus the oppressive weight of the people of Paris, Louis XIV sought isolation in his Court and in the gardens of Versailles. The Louvre remained unfinished. The exterior decoration was only in the preliminary stages and even the roofing had not been completed.

Every part that could be inhabited was then used by royal administrative offices, courtesans and mostly by the academies and appointed artists. The finest apartments were reserved for the sessions held by the different academies: the Académie Française, the academies of art and sculpture, of the sciences and the humanities. Entire libraries and collections were stored there.

The art academy gave classes and organized exhibitions of works by members; these were displayed in part of the Grande Galerie and in the adjoining Salon Carré (square salon). Hence, by the 18th century, the exhibition held every two years, which had become the highlight of artistic life in Paris, was known as the "Salon" after the Salon Carré.

The 18th century was not an auspicious time for the Louvre and recriminations were heard from enlightened men indignant at state neglect of the palace. Under Louis XV, a half-hearted effort cleared the Cour Carrée of its houses and had one of the pediments sculpted.

The overriding concern of the great minds of the time was the plan for a museum at the Louvre to display the royal collections. The master of buildings under Louis XVI, the Comte d'Angiviller, gave his full endorsement to the project.

A Museum, first National,
then Napoleonic

a museum finally came into existence in the Louvre with the French Revolution. In 1792 the decision was made to open the palace to the public and this was done on August 10, 1793, the date marking the anniversary of the fall of the monarchy. Initially, only paintings, objets d'art and busts relating to the nation were exhibited in the Grande Galerie, while the Salon was for contemporary artists. By November it had become a permanent institution.

The museum became richer with the addition of royal collections, possessions seized from emigrants and property confiscated from the Church. Revolutionary armies that had been rampaging through Europe brought back quite extraordinary booty with works of art from Belgium, Germany, and in particular from Italy.

In 1797, with the treaty of Tolentino, the Louvre received masterpieces from the Vatican, including works by Raphael and famous antiquities. Napoleon Bonaparte, a young general at the time, had been influential in the initial decision that had led to such military enrichment. In 1799 the apartment of Anne of Austria was turned into a museum for antiquities.

A succession of rooms were opened up and supporting walls replaced with columns taken from Charlemagne's rotunda in Aachen. Bonaparte gave his approval for the museum to bear his name.

Later, as Emperor, Napoleon jealously guarded "his museum". As the residence was the Tuileries palace, he returned to previous royal plans to extend the Louvre to join the Tuileries and appointed Pierre Fontaine and Charles Percier as architects in charge. Stonemasons were brought in and work was begun on a new wing along the rue de Rivoli, a recent addition to the streets of Paris. The vertical section facing the garden to the west (a copy of the section of the Grande Galerie built by Henry IV) is still standing, but on the eastern side the circular Saint Napoleon chapel has disappeared. The most visible part of the extensive work carried out under Napoleon is the exterior decoration of the palace: the Triumphal Arch of the Carrousel, built in honour of the army in 1806, forms the gateway to the Tuileries courtyard and is decorated with large marble sculptures illustrating the Napoleonic campaigns.

In the centre of the Colonnade, on the pediments of the Cour Carrée, elaborate relief sculptures honour the sovereign protector of the arts. Inside, Percier and Fontaine built grand staircases on either side of the Colonnade as well as the staircase leading to the museum. What remains today are the rooms named after Percier and Fontaine, their marble columns contrasting harmoniously with the opulence of the sculpted decoration.

Museums at the Time
of the Restoration

With the fall of the Empire in 1815, the allied powers demanded the return of booty plundered in Europe. This meant masterpieces were to be given back to their rightful owners. To fill the empty spaces, works were brought from other residences. The department of antiquities was given Greek vases and new acquisitions including the *Venus de Milo*, a gift made to Louis XVIII in 1821. And more new sections were opened.

Renaissance and modern sculpture moved into a gallery on the ground floor of the Cour Carrée, superbly decorated by Fontaine. Today it houses the collection of Oriental antiquities. Art works from the Middle Ages were displayed in a special room for precious objets d'art.

The most important innovation was the Egyptian museum, established under the control of Champollion, the man famous for having deciphered hieroglyphics. Acquisitions included pieces and sculptures collected in Egypt, in particular those brought back by Salt and Drovetti. Charles X had this now royal museum located on the first floor of the south wing of the Cour Carrée.

A succession of richly coloured rooms led from the Hall of Columns, so named because of its fluted white columns. Pieces were displayed in tall mahogany cases and the ceilings above were the work of the finest artists of the time, including Ingres. The hall was also richly decorated with stucco work and fireplaces embellished with bronze.

This group of rooms, designed for both the Roman and Egyptian collections, is currently reserved for the Egyptian department. Ceramics from ancient times are displayed in the parallel gallery on the southern side, which was decorated in a similarly lavish style at a later date.

The sovereigns did not, however, forget the palatial ambition of the Louvre, which was to form one vast edifice with the Tuileries, the official residence. Work was continued on the north wing along the rue de Rivoli; the unfinished bull's-eyes in the Cour Carrée were decorated, and two vast, grandiose halls were created in the Louvre.

The hall for royal audiences, used for meetings of the Chambers, was directly above the Caryatid Hall (which now houses the collection of Greek bronzes). Adjoining this was a series of rooms which is now the department of objets d'art; at the time it was the hall for the Council of State. Once again painted ceilings feature subjects glorifying the monarchy and, with their rich tones, add a certain warmth.

The "New Louvre"
of Napoleon III

the 1848 Revolution, dated March 24, 1848 by decree, proclaimed that "the Louvre must be completed", that it was "the people's palace". This noble ambition won the support of Victor Hugo who, in a speech to the Assembly, declared that the Louvre must become a "Mecca of Intelligence". Plans to extend the Louvre to join the Tuileries were drawn up. Priority was given to restoration work that was urgently needed in the Grande and Petite Galeries. The architect Duban restored the façade of the Grande Galerie, and in particular the Galerie d'Apollon, which was in a state of virtual ruin. He renovated the decor and had Delacroix paint a most impressive work, *The Triumph of Apollo*, a romantic composition with remarkable effects of light, yet reminiscent of the spirit of the "Grand Siècle". To offer a palatial setting for the collection of paintings, Duban devised the decor for the two main Salons that housed the museum's masterpieces. The Salon Carré contained the finest paintings from all periods and all countries; the complementary Salon of the Seven Fireplaces was devoted to contemporary French artists.

The ceilings in both Salons show the work of sculptors and stucco artists respecting the same traditions as in the Galerie d'Apollon, with large white figures set against a gold background. The two Salons, inaugurated by the "Prince-President" in 1851, foreshadowed even more radical change for the palace. Louis-Napoleon Bonaparte, soon to become Napoleon III, had found his own inspiration in plans for the Republic. His official residence was at the Tuileries palace and his aim was to transform the vast Louvre-Tuileries complex to create an imperial city. From 1852 to 1857, the architects Visconti (who died in 1853) and then Lefuel carried out extensive construction work designed to bring about the longed-for meeting of the Louvre and the Tuileries on the rue de Rivoli. The residential area still standing between the two palaces was demolished and a series of wings and courtyards were built, enclosed within a circle of tall pavilions named after the leading servants of the state: Denon, Richelieu, Colbert, Turgot, Sully and Mollien. The whole structure radiated around a central quadrangle — the Cour Napoléon. The architect Lefuel included allusions to earlier Louvre features and styles (bull's-eyes, caryatids, trophies, attic levels) and adorned the façades with lavish sculptures. The finest artists were called in: Barye sculpted the pediment on the Sully Pavilion and the principal groups of sculptures on the Richelieu and Denon Pavilions. More than three hundred sculptors worked under the supervision of Rude, Préault, Carpeaux, Guillaume, Duret and Simart. The terraces were occupied by no fewer than eighty-three statues of eminent figures (all French, no women, no soldiers) representing the arts, literature, the Church and the state. The military were relegated to niches along the rue de Rivoli. In 1861 Lefuel embarked on a campaign to destroy part of the old Louvre and replace it with new buildings, featuring, of course, profuse ornamentation. The old Flore Pavilion and more than one third of the Grande Galerie were razed and replaced by a new Flore Pavilion, a larger wing to hold the sessions of the Assemblies, and the main entrance gates opening towards the Seine. This was just one step; Lefuel's plan was for an ongoing process of regeneration, but he was stopped by the outbreak of war and the fall of the Empire.

Inside the new imperial city the museum had gained ground. Some of the new rooms were luxuriously decorated: for example, the Hall of the Emperors which housed ancient sculptures but also celebrated the modern, victorious Emperors, Napoleon III, who was in power at the time, and his uncle. Part of the Grande Galerie disappeared only to be rebuilt and lavishly decorated in 1869 with the addition of two rotundas graced with voluptuous female bacchanals shaped in stucco by Rodin's master, Carrier-Belleuse. Lefuel devoted special efforts to areas used for imperial pomp and circumstance: staircases, ministries and official halls.

the State Room, used for extraordinary meetings of the Chambers when the Emperor presided, was in the heart of the museum. While the decor has not survived, there is still the Denon Salon, which is the vestibule with a vaulted ceiling rising to an apex above large *trompe-l'oeil* draperies. The artist Charles-Louis Müller depicted the generous patronage of the arts offered by the French sovereigns by painting groups of artists and allegories of the arts. Beneath the State Room, the great Riding Academy, used for horse-riding displays for the Imperial Prince, was connected to various stables and grooms' lodgings, which have now been turned into rooms belonging to the museum.

In this enumeration of official activities, special mention must be made of the prestigious apartments of the Minister of State. A grand and important figure at Court, he was the intermediary between the Emperor and the Chambers and also responsible for the management of grand building projects of the state. The first to hold the title, Achille Fould, chose to see his residence as a reflection and display of his power. Gold shone from room to room in an uninterrupted series of reception areas: Grand Salon, theatre salon, small dining room, large dining room, and so on. The result was the continuation of one of the greatest single examples of the decorative opulence of the Second Empire. Under Napoleon III, the Louvre also became a palace of staircases, although the grand staircase to the museum, where visitors today can see the *Winged Victory of Samothrace*, had not been completed at the time; the extremely ambitious structure was the work of Lefuel. The architect did indeed decorate a variety of staircases: the Mollien staircase leading to halls where paintings are hung; today's "Lefuel staircase" that led to the imperial library, resplendent with cleverly designed double spirals; the Minister's staircase leading to his apartments, with dazzling chandeliers and columns; and the Flore staircase, of which only the upper level was decorated to Lefuel's instructions after the fall of the Empire.

The Victory of the Museum

the fall of the Empire and the end of the political role of the Louvre came at the same time. In May 1871, the Tuileries palace was set on fire, the flames lit by members of the Commune as the culmination of a week of blood and violence. The charred superstructure survived but was never restored. For ideological reasons it was decided to demolish the palace and this was done in 1882, thereby removing any visible sign of past monarchies. In theory, the museum remained as master of the domain, together with some administrative offices in the Flore Pavilion and the Richelieu wing, which in 1872 had become the home of the Ministry of Finance. Gradually the collections grew and the museum was given the Pavilion of the States (1900), the Flore wing (1910), the Flore Pavilion (1964), and the Richelieu wing, the latter finally being vacated by the Ministry of Finance in 1989.

To improve presentation and displays, the museum needed to be reorganized and rearranged in an architectural style both handsome and functional. First there was the great campaign of the 1930s. Begun in 1926 and interrupted by the war, it consisted of a total reorganization of various departments: Oriental antiquities, sculpture and some Egyptian art pieces. The modern style with clean lines was designed by the architect Ferran, whose name was given to the *Winged Victory* staircase. The overall enterprise was completed between 1950 and 1980. When the "Finance" or Richelieu wing was returned to the Louvre, with the transfers to the Orsay Museum in 1986, the 19th-century plans inevitably required new and radical changes. This was the project that came to be known as the "Grand Louvre", the final metamorphosis introducing logical planning and itineraries for all departments. This onerous task became the responsibility of the public building commission for the Grand Louvre.

The first stage, managed by the Chinese-American architect I.M. Pei, was the building of the Pyramid, a vast web of glass and steel set above a large, naturally lit, open hall. Less visible to the general public was the work beneath the Cour Napoléon: technical facilities, an auditorium, temporary exhibition areas and halls presenting the history of the Louvre, plus public facilities such as a book shop and restaurants. The second stage coincided with the celebration of the bicentenary of the museum in November 1993. The Richelieu wing was finally opened to the public and now houses the collection of Oriental antiquities, together with a reproduction of the Assyrian palace of Sargon in Khorsabad and Islamic antiquities, previously kept in extremely limited quarters. Glassed-in courtyards cast natural light on the collection of French statues; objets d'art are superbly lit, Flemish and Dutch paintings are now together in the Rubens Luxembourg gallery; and French artists on the second floor form a passage from the Richelieu wing right around the Cour Carrée. The grand staircase in the Richelieu wing and the sky-lights in the courtyards, together with the Carrousel boutiques set around the inside of the Pyramid, now constitute one of the latest architectural innovations for a monument that has lived through the major artistic changes of the past eight centuries.

PRINCIPAUX DONATEURS
LES AMIS DU LOUVRE
SOCIÉTÉ FONDÉE EN 1897

The Louvre

The Pyramid by I.M. Pei (1988), reflecting the façade of the Richelieu Pavilion sculpted under the supervision of Hector-Martin Lefuel (1856–57).
The groups by Antoine-Louis Barye, depicting Peace and Order, on either side of the imperial arms, are copies of the originals (1988).

The roof of the Marsan Pavilion made to the plans of Hector-Martin Lefuel (1875).
Antoine-François Gérard, *France Victorious* (1809), stone statue on a pedestal standing sentry at the Triumphal Arch of the Carrousel. One of the four statues that once stood along the fence of the Tuileries palace.

The Colonnade by Claude Perrault and François d'Orbay (1667–74): a series of double Corinthian columns.

N, the emblem of Napoleon I and Napoleon III, seen on the ironwork of the palace and here on the eastern entrance to the Louvre.

Napoleon I had his architects decorate the palace of Louis XIV. **Victory on a Horse-drawn Chariot** shown distributing wreaths: tympanum sculpted by Pierre Cartellier (1808) in the main arched passage of the Colonnade wing. Originally inspired by an ancient painting.

The crystalline effect of the glass panels of the Pyramid highlights the ornate decoration of the Napoleon III period. **The Denon Pavilion seen through the Pyramid.** The decoration, sculpted under the supervision of Hector-Martin Lefuel (1856-57), features caryatids by Brian and Jacquot and a pediment by Simart.

The Louvre is a museum of staircases, from the 16th-century Lescot staircase to the grand creations of Lefuel, the last of the architects respecting such traditions. The Pei **Pyramid** (1988) features a **spiral staircase** with an elevator rising to form a column in the centre.

Cour Marly: glassed in and redesigned by I.M. Pei and Michel Macary (1993). Statues originally in the Marly gardens at the time of Louis XIV have been arranged in a setting of white stone from Burgundy, with rubber plants from California.

Cour Marly. Standing out against the glass, a Marly horse, made by Guillaume Coustou for the trough at the Château de Marly (1739–45). Formerly subjected to the harshest treatment in Paris standing on the Place de la Concorde, the group became part of the museum in 1984.

The museum has always endeavoured to produce the best conditions for its masterpieces: for example, the **Winged Victory**, standing on the Daru staircase, constructed by Hector-Martin Lefuel (1855–57) and later modified by Albert Ferran (1934).

The Lefuel staircase in the Richelieu wing, originally built by Hector-Martin Lefuel (1855–59) for the imperial library, manifests the architectural concerns of its day, hollowing out walls to form great arches and combining qualities of lightness and immortality.

Grand Salon in the apartments of Napoleon III, decorated for the Ministry of State by Hector-Martin Lefuel (1859–60). Paintings by Maréchal. From 1872 to 1989 it housed the Ministry of Finance. Reception rooms feature stucco work with gold highlights, a perfect contrast for the colourful paintings.

Grand dining room in the apartments of Napoleon III, decorated for the Ministry of State by Hector-Martin Lefuel (1859–60).

Small apartments dating from the time of Napoleon III.

The large Denon Salon. Under the supervision of Hector-Martin Lefuel, Charles-Louis Müller painted the walls and ceilings while Alexandre Oliva created the sculptures (1864–66).

The Hall of Columns, by Pierre-François Fontaine (1820), in the south wing of the Cour Carrée (formerly the Queen's apartment).

The consultation room of the department of the graphic arts, seen from the top of the staircase once built to take the sovereigns to the Flore Pavilion but never completed. Decoration carried out under the supervision of Hector-Martin Lefuel by A. Cabanel (painting) and Eugène Guillaume (sculpture) (1869–72). The restoration work and new presentation date from 1968.

The Rotunda of Apollo: *The Fall of Icarus* by Merry-Joseph Blondel (centre), *The Elements* by Couder in the compartments, and grisaille paintings by Jean-Baptiste Mauzaisse (1818–21).

The Grande Galerie: in the foreground the rotunda rebuilt by Lefuel, with a decorative cupola by Albert-Ernest Carrier-Belleuse (1869–70).

The Galerie d'Apollon rebuilt in 1662 is the first example of the grand decorative art style of the period of Louis XIV. **Two details of stucco work** by François Girardon made for the Galerie d'Apollon under the supervision of Charles Lebrun (1662–64).

Abundance by Merry-Joseph Blondel, arching of the ceiling in a room in the western wing of the Cour Carrée, decorated for the Council of State (1827).

Georges Braque, *Les Oiseaux*, decoration on the ceiling of the Henry II vestibule, dating from 1953 — a bid to combine the old and the new; the frame dates from the 16th century.

The Rotunda of Mars: stucco work by the Marsy brothers (1658), under the supervision of Charles Errard during the reign of Louis XIV. The medallions by Bernard Lange and Lorta depicting the arts were commissioned in 1801, as was the medallion beneath the arch symbolising the union of the three arts by Antoine-Louis Chaudet. The central fresco by Jean-Baptiste Mauzaisse, *Prometheus Giving Fire to Man*, dates from 1826 and is a copy of a work by Jean-Simon Berthélémy (1802).

Vaulted ceiling of the Riding Academy. Decorated in 1861 by Frémiet, Rouillard, Jacquemont, Demay and Houguenade under the supervision of Hector-Martin Lefuel. The capitals feature symbols of riding and hunting with horses' heads (right) and bears' heads (left). Since 1989 it has housed ancient statues that have been restored, in particular coloured marble sculptures.

The Hall of Caryatids. Construction by Pierre Lescot. Caryatids sculpted by Jean Goujon in 1550 support the musicians' stage at the far end.

The grand southern staircase in the Colonnade by Charles Percier and Pierre Fontaine. The tympanum on the right depicting justice is the work of Antoine-François Gérard.

The Hall of Augustus, originally the Hall of the Emperors, decorated by Hector-Martin Lefuel. The ceiling painted by Matout shows the assembly of the gods. Stucco work by Duchoiselle depicts the victories of emperors in ancient times.

The apartment of Anne of Austria (1654–56) was rearranged to house the museum of antiquities; columns from Aachen were added in 1799.

The Hall of Saint Louis, the lower hall in the medieval Louvre beneath the western wing. The outside walls date from the time of Philip Augustus. The central columns and piers of the arches were rebuilt in the mid-13th century. The walls and low vaulted ceilings seen far left were added in the 16th century when Pierre Lescot built a staircase for the new Renaissance wing (1546). Recent restoration work was done in 1989 by Richard Peduzzi.

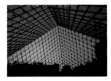

The Pyramid by I.M. Pei (1988). Classical in form, in daylight its glass walls reflect the historic façades and by night it illuminates the Cour Napoléon.

The façade of the Cour Napoléon, by Hector-Martin Lefuel (1854–57). The architect added lavish sculpted ornamentation to the basic classical structure inspired by the earlier style of the Louvre.

Statues of famous men on the terrace of the Turgot wing in the Cour Napoléon. Plans by Hector-Martin Lefuel (1854–57) were designed to celebrate the glory of France's illustrious men. Left to right: Colbert by Gayrard, Mazarin by Herbert (père), Georges Buffon by Cudiné, Froissard by Lemaire and Jean-Jacques Rousseau by Farochon.

The Eastern Pavilion on the Cour Carrée, seen through the main entrance to the Sully Pavilion. The pediment is the work of Guillaume Coustou, made to the plans of Ange-Jacques Gabriel (1757). The upper part of the wing on the other side of the Colonnade was completed during the reign of Louis XV.

The arrangement of the layout in tiers reveals the vast diversity of the Louvre: in the foreground the **Triumphal Arch of the Carrousel** by Charles Percier and Pierre Fontaine (1806); behind, the **Pyramid** by I.M. Pei (1988) and, in the distance, the **Sully Pavilion** built by Jacques Le Mercier at the time of Louis XIII, later redecorated by Hector-Martin Lefuel (1856–57).

The publisher wishes
to express his gratitude to
Mr. Michel Laclotte,
Président Honoraire of the Louvre
Museum, for his invaluable
assistance in the preparation
of this book.